Questions on Dressage

Questions on Dressage

LÉONIE M. MARSHALL

J. A. Allen
London

British Library Cataloguing-in-Publication Data.
A catalogue record for this book is available from the British Library

ISBN 0.85131.632.8

Published in Great Britain in 1996 by
J. A. Allen & Company Limited,
1 Lower Grosvenor Place, Buckingham Palace Road,
London, SW1W 0EL

Typeset by Textype Typesetters, Cambridge
Printed by Dah Hua Printing Press Co., Hong Kong

Designed by Judy Linard

First printed 1989
Revised edition 1996

Contents

5

Introduction

Over the years, beginners, novice riders trying to school their horses in basic obedience, people aspiring to ride dressage, and riders with horses with difficult problems, have asked a variety of questions regarding training.

In this book I have endeavoured to give some answers which are comprehensible and concise and all of which have been tried and proved by experts.

Reference may have to be made to textbooks regarding aids and description of exercises, etc., but the idea of this book was to give the rider a course to action to take, which he may, through lack of knowledge or experience, have been unable to work out for himself.

As with all things, there is more than one route to get where you are going, but having decided upon one, stick to it, and you stand a chance of arrival!

Léonie Marshall

Short dressage arena (20 m × 40 m)

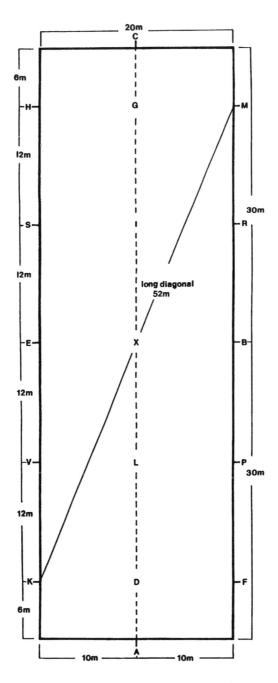

Long dressage arena (20 m ×60 m)

11

Question

Could you advise me as to the type of horse I should buy if I want to compete in dressage competitions and do I need to have a Hanoverian?

ANSWER

A good deal depends on whether you desire to compete at the top, or whether your ambition is more modest. A top horse is hard to find and expensive to buy, but there are many different types that can go quite a long way and give their riders considerable success. There are some general qualities you might look for:

1. Head joined to neck in such a way that gives plenty of room to allow flexion.
2. Naturally cresty neck coming up out of the withers.
3. A short back, but not too short.
4. Rounded strong quarters with hind legs built underneath them.
5. Good bone and substance. Good length of stride and freedom of shoulders.
6. A slightly rounded action of the foreleg (as seen from the side) and naturally active action of the joints of the hind legs.
7. Straight action is preferable, but not absolutely essential. This can be seen from either in front or behind when the horse is in motion.
8. A willing but equable temperament is an enormous help.
9. Height should be decided according to the size, shape and ability of the rider. It is really no good choosing an enormous horse if the rider is only 1.37 m (4 ft 6 in) or is inclined to be plump! Nor should a novice rider choose something which may look right for the job, but which

they cannot handle.

As rider and horse will probably have many years together, it is important to choose something suitable which can be enjoyed and not be exhausting or frustrating because of its unwillingness or poor temperament.

We cannot all buy the horse we would really like, but there are horses around who have a lot of ability in their way, and who, if correctly and systematically trained, will have a lot of success.

Question

I own a Thoroughbred mare and she seems to become tense and overexcited, resisting in all sorts of ways every new thing I try to teach her. Is she unsuitable for dressage?

ANSWER

Unfortunately without seeing her I cannot really tell you, but Thoroughbreds are a law unto themselves, and a knowledge of the way they react mentally and physically is essential if you are going to try to train them. Excitability is certainly not an ideal temperament for dressage because of the difficulty in obtaining sufficient calmness for the brain to be receptive to learning.

A great deal of patience is required to train such horses, the rider having to accept the fact that it will all take a good deal longer than with a horse of equable nature.

It is impossible to train a horse, particularly for such a precise discipline as dressage, without exact control by the legs and hands of the rider. This in itself can be hard to do on a horse whose excitability leads it to nervous tension at any kind of real control. It can be done, but will certainly be a challenge, taking years rather than months.

The other factor regarding excitable horses is that of the rider, who will require a firm quiet seat and steady hands. Any looseness in the saddle, poor contact, lack of co-ordination or inconsistency of aids will upset and confuse the horse, which may result in excitability or resistance.

There are many horses who are classed as excitable or very resistant, but a good deal, or all, of it could be reduced by knowledge and better riding.

Question

I have a very lazy horse who I find I cannot get going. Have you any suggestions?

ANSWER
Without seeing the horse it is difficult to judge whether he is lazy by nature, as some are, or whether he is lazy owing to lack of knowledge or acceptance of the aids. If it is the former, it will be difficult to change his character, so maybe you will need to use him for something which he enjoys, e.g. jumping, hunting or hacking. If it is the latter, which can probably only be ascertained by someone with experience of different types of horses, you will need to work on making him go forward from the leg aids. A schooling whip and possibly spurs may have to be used because he will need to learn to respect the leg and answer a squeeze; constant kicking by the rider does not command respect.

If he should kick out, buck or nap to the stick, careful and firmer use of the whip will have to be employed. Sometimes this can be distressing for the rider but seldom for the horse: they have very thick skins!

Determination by the rider will ultimately triumph over stubbornness by the horse, which seems only reasonable, since we have them for our pleasure!

Feeding and work can play a part in making horses more willing because a fit horse on suitable short feeds will be able to work better and harder then one which is filled up with bulk, or worked inconsistently.

Question

I have been told that I should 'ride my horse in' each day before starting work. Could you explain what this means and how long it should last?

ANSWER

Riding-in means loosening up the horse and preparing him for the harder work to follow. If he has come straight from the stable he may be a little stiff and his muscles will need time to warm up and become elastic. The length of time for riding-in will depend upon how quickly this happens, and of course each horse will vary in this respect.

The time could be divided as follows. Begin with walk on a long rein round the school with changes of direction. I personally do not agree with a loose rein because I think that the horse should accept a contact from the start, although he will be allowed to stretch, and go forwards and down to the bit.

Then, work in rising trot on a long rein to allow the back to come free and round. Include some large circles.

Continue with canter in the same way.

Finish the riding-in with a walk on a free rein to allow complete relaxation mentally and physically before the commencement of the lesson.

Question

For how long should I ride-in at a show?

ANSWER

Unfortunately it is impossible to give an exact answer. This is a problem puzzling to most people and the only way to find out is by trial and error. All horses react so differently to show conditions.

There are, however, a few guidelines to follow. Unless he is very laid back, your horse will probably need to have a good look at the show surroundings, so time should be set aside for this. If he is an excitable type it may be preferable to let him settle on the lunge rather than ride him and risk having a tiring time which will wear both of you out. Because of extra tension, a little more time than usual may be needed to loosen up before you start really expecting him to work. When you start to work him, bear in mind that excitability gives false impulsion so you must work him for enough time to ensure that he will let you really ride him. Too little time spent working may not dampen the excitement enough. Once his excitement is over he may very quickly go cold on the whole idea so a short rest may be needed before getting down to the real warming up.

There are certain things you have to do so it may help to work the timing backwards from when you know you are in the arena. For instance, a minute to go round the arena before the bell, three minutes to remove the horse's boots if used for working in, and put on your jacket if necessary. Another couple of minutes to go over the test mentally. Two minutes to get to the arena from the riding-in area, 20 or 30 minutes to work the horse quite hard, five minutes walking about following loosening period, 10 minutes loosening up, 10 minutes on the lunge. Within this time period there should be a formula which will suit your horse, although there will always be some that will need longer riding-in than others.

Question
Do I do the same exercises every day?

ANSWER
In order to establish a new exercise in the horse's mind, repetition is important. Whatever is worked upon one day needs a follow-up the day after, and probably for several consecutive days. Once it is clear and the horse willingly and easily gives to the aids of that exercise, it may be repeated at greater intervals. The exercises the horse already knows will probably be part of the general routine and will be used towards the build-up of the training.

However, although suppling, straightening and overall work on aids acceptance is necessary each day, I do not believe that the horse should necessarily be made to work through everything he knows every day. There is usually some particular thing you want to improve. Exercises should be used to this end, and when sufficient improvement on that point is made, the lesson may end for that day.

Question
If I am having a problem with an exercise, should I carry on until I get it perfect?

ANSWER
Bearing in mind the supreme difficulty in obtaining perfection, it is probably wiser to accept only improvements. Sometimes you have to settle for very small ones and be satisfied. With any problem it may be important to struggle for a while in order to make progress. It would be helpful to assess whether the problem is caused by naughtiness or confusion.

If it is naughtiness then you should pursue the matter until the horse will accept what he is being asked and some distinct improvement is attained.

If it is confusion, then the horse will be upset and tense. It is not easy to be receptive in this condition so it may be as well to back off, to a degree, or even to change the exercise, temporarily. Then give time to reconsider your approach. Mostly, quiet perseverance overcomes the problem and will get you some way towards the ultimate goal.

Question
How many days a week shall I school?

ANSWER
It depends on each individual horse, his temperament and attitude. I think every horse deserves one day off a week.

Some feel quite neglected if they do not work six days a week because they actually enjoy working. The ones who find it rather heavy going are best schooled every other day. Alternatively, school for three days running and then hack or do some other activity. When teaching a new exercise the continuity is important, so you may need to work for several consecutive days and then have a break.

With a young horse, allowance should be made for limited physical capacity for some time. He can learn new things quickly, but will need time to develop his muscles. Trained horses do not need the daily repetition unless they are competing a lot when it will be important to keep them supple and obedient to detail.

Each rider must get to know his horse and train according to the animal's energies.

Question
How long should I school for each day?

ANSWER
No-one can say exactly because every horse is so different, and a lot depends on whether everything is going well or whether you are struggling with a problem. However, as a rough guide, I would say about an hour, but a quarter of an hour or so is for loosening the horse, and ten minutes or so at the end is for cooling off, so the lesson would be half an hour or a little more. Some days it may well be less, if a particular lesson has been achieved well in a short time.

There is no point in keeping to a set time for the sake of it because the important point is to teach the horse what he has to do. If he grasps it quickly, take him back to the stable or go for a hack. He will remember the exercise best in this way.

You do not have to go through an entire routine every day, when the horse is learning.

Question
How do I finish my schooling session each day?

ANSWER
I think there are two points to consider. Firstly, it is impor-

tant for the horse to finish on a good note, whatever the length of time you have been schooling. Try to end with something you especially want the horse to remember the next time.

Secondly, the horse will need to cool off physically and relax mentally, so a short period of time should be spent in a free, forward rising trot, allowing the horse to stretch, and then a free walk on a long rein, after which he should be brought to a correct square halt on the aids, before you dismount.

Question
I am told that my horse has wolf teeth. Is this why he tosses his head a lot?

ANSWER
Tossing heads are rarely caused by wolf teeth, but are much more likely to be due to poor co-ordination of the rider's hands and legs, and lack of discipline to the aids. Occasionally wolf teeth may interfere with the position of the bit, so, if your horse has them, it may be worth getting the vet to check on this for you.

I know vets who say that they remove wolf teeth mostly to please the owner, not because they really are going to make any difference. Sharp teeth are probably more likely to cause trouble, so it is wise to have the horse's mouth checked at least once a year.

Question
I can't carry a stick as my horse is terrified of them. Shall I use spurs?

ANSWER
I have come across this problem many times and, so far, I have not found a horse who will not accept a schooling whip eventually, if properly used.

The problem is presumably caused by the horse having had a beating, either in the stable or when ridden, for some specific reason. Sometimes it is not possible to carry a whip initially if the horse is very nervous. Give him time to get to know you and realise that you are not going to hurt him.

Once he begins to gain confidence, take a short whip and carry it on one side only. After a few days, change it to the other hand. When he is used to this, change it from one hand to the other, very quietly, in halt. After a day or two try this in walk, and so on.

How long you need to do this before trying the whole procedure again with a schooling whip will depend on the horse's reaction. Try to choose a fairly stiff whip because anything that flaps at the end could cause a problem; they tend to flick the horse when you don't want them to.

When the horse accepts you carrying the whip, the next step is to teach him to let you use it to aid the leg. This should be approached by degrees. First, in halt, rest the whip on the horse's flank just behind the leg and soothe him with the voice. Then stroke him gently with the end of it, still behind the leg. He will soon accept this when he realises nothing terrible is going to happen. After a few days, try a gentle tap. He will probably jump forwards, but of course that is the reaction you want as long as it is not followed by panic.

It may take some months before it is possible to use the whip as it should be used to make the horse more responsive, and therefore lighter to the leg aids. During this time the horse's training will progress and he will become more obedient.

With the greater control, the use of the whip will become easier. I do not believe that you can satisfactorily train a horse without the aid of a schooling whip, its help is required in many ways. It is, therefore, important to teach the horse to accept it.

I do not find that spurs are a substitute so would not recommend using them instead.

Question

I have noticed a lot of dressage riders wearing spurs. Should I wear them and, if so, when do I start?

ANSWER

Much depends on the type of horse you have and the reason for wearing them; the latter point being the most important.

Spurs are not actually required to be worn in dressage competitions until medium standard, but should be introduced at home before that to allow the horse to become accustomed to them.

They should not be worn in order to coerce the horse into going forward, but are intended to enable the rider to use a finer aid. Prodding and poking at the horse's sides is incorrect and frequently dulls the leg aid instead of making it more effective. It may make the horse very resentful and even nappy. Many riders do use spurs instead of making their horse answer a light aid by reinforcing it with the schooling whip.

Some very lazy horses may need a spur as well as the leg and whip but, if that is their nature, they are not very suitable for dressage. Excitable horses will take longer to accept the feel of a spur, and will only do so when they totally accept the rider's leg aids.

Question

My horse is young and untrained, should I rise or sit when I am schooling in trot?

ANSWER

In principle, rising trot is probably better for a young horse's back. This leaves the muscles free and allows him the chance to round rather than hollow his back. This is important because it prevents the tension that causes stiffness and, eventually, resistance. Most riders will rise anyway at the warming-up stage of a schooling session to allow the horse to 'free' himself.

Experts with good established positions may subsequently decide to sit, quite a bit. If the seat is less secure, damage can be done to the horse's back by bumping about inadvertently.

Question
My horse carries his head too high. Is it all right to use running (draw) reins to get it down?

ANSWER
There are times when it may be necessary to employ the assistance of running reins temporarily, either because the conventional method simply will not work, or for some particular exercise. This is normally only necessary if the horse's mouth is thoroughly spoiled, if he has developed very strong muscle under his neck from having been allowed to go above the bit, or if he is a very big, tough horse who continually uses his strength against the rider.

I do think it is preferable to try to achieve submission by using the legs and hands, and teaching the horse to soften his mouth by patience and using suppling exercises, i.e. flexions, shoulder-in, etc.

Question
I usually jump my horse in a martingale. Should I take it off to school him?

ANSWER
I think you should try. Any additional piece of equipment used reduces the true effect of the legs and hands with which we really want to achieve a result. Temporary use of gadgets can be very helpful if all else has failed. It also depends on how they are fitted.

Standing martingales have no training value at all. Running martingales can sometimes be of assistance with an older horse, if he has learned to get very much above the bit. However, if they are too tight they will tend to drag the head down into an overbent position as the hind legs are driven up. Also, there is a danger that riders will use it only to get the head down *without* driving the hind legs up. In this case the horse will usually revert to the above the bit position when the martingale is removed.

Question
When should I put my horse into a double bridle?

ANSWER
It depends on what you want to do.

Many riders want to show as well as do dressage, and the 'dress' for the class may require a double bridle, in which case it may have to be introduced earlier than it would if the rider were doing solely dressage. Either way, I believe that the horse should be quite happy, accepting the aids in the various gaits and transitions, and be knowledgeable about bend before any other bit is introduced. Then he may be ridden in the double, either in the school, or out hacking, but with more accent on the bradoon.

There is an often held misconception regarding the curb chain. A loose curb chain is not doing the horse a kindness because it allows far too much leverage of the arm of the bit. A tighter chain will be rather like having air brakes, but if used carefully will enable the rider to use more refined aids.

A double bridle is not required in dressage competitions until advanced standard, although it may be used from elementary upwards.

Horses should be able to do all the Grand Prix movements in a snaffle, but are required to do the tests in a double.

The double bridle is used for containing the gradually increasing impulsion and collection, so, until you are reaching this stage, there is no particular point in introducing it.

Question

Should my horse be on the bit out hacking?

ANSWER
I think that the important point to remember is that if the horse is to become trained, the aids must be consistent. The rider should also realise that the horse can either be on the bit or on a loose rein and that there is nothing in between!

It is possible to ride on a long rein on the bit or on a short rein on the bit, but any inconsistent contact will result in a hard mouth and unsteady head.

I would say in answer to the question, therefore, that if you are to enjoy a hack (which most people do for relaxation) but still be safe, it is best to do part of the ride on the bit on a short rein, and the remainder on the bit on a long rein.

I would like to draw attention to the fact that trotting or cantering, especially in the company of others, can be dangerous unless the horse is controlled. He can only be truly controlled if he is on the bit.

Question
Should my horse have a holiday, and for how long?

ANSWER
No doubt opinions vary about holidays. I believe that a long break allows the dressage horse to become too slack and lose his muscle tone. This can cause difficulties in maintaining the required suppleness.

Mentally, the horse may need a break from concentrated learning and it may be better to give short breaks more frequently. For example, early spring, mid-summer and autumn, for no longer than one week at a time.

He can be turned out for a few hours each day to rest, but not turned away, as an eventer would be. If the horse is turned away, owners must be prepared to bring the horse back slowly in order to get him fit again, and to return muscles to full working order.

Question
Is it possible for any horse to learn dressage, or do you have to have a particular type?

ANSWER
The answer to this is that you can certainly train any horse to do dressage, but some will have a limit which may fall far short of Grand Prix.

There will be those who can be trained up to Grand Prix level but, owing to conformation difficulties or lack of stride, will never be brilliant.

The horses most likely to do well will start with good conformation and a naturally good stride and temperament. Those horses who are exceedingly idle or very nervous will be unlikely to progress far. A horse with very upright shoulders will probably not have much freedom of movement. Others who are long in the back will have more difficulty in engaging their hindquarters, as will those who are high behind.

Most horses can achieve the majority of dressage movements, but riders should be aware of their shortcomings and limitations, only expecting brilliance from a really talented horse.

Question
My horse takes very short steps in walk, is there anything I can do?

ANSWER
It depends upon what sort of walk your horse does naturally when he is loose in the field. Some horses are not blessed with a long walk stride, so with the best will in the world there is very little that can be done.

However, some horses do shorten up when ridden. They may do this because they are restricted by their rider, probably the most common reason, or they may get shorter because they are hurrying too much and overbalancing.

I think the first thing to do, having established that the stride is naturally long, is to walk on a long rein. Allow the horse complete freedom to take his maximum length stride. If he hurries, restrain him, and then give the rein, until he will walk slowly, without contact. Gradually then begin to make contact, ensuring that you do not restrict the horse at all. If he remains calm it should gradually be possible to use the legs to squeeze him forwards to the contact, which can then begin to bring him onto the bit.

It will be a help to the horse's relaxation if you relax your own seat muscles and allow yourself and the horse to swing along together. Any tension from you will make him tighten his back muscles which will probably result in a shortening of the steps.

Question

What can I do to make my horse lengthen his neck in the free walk?

ANSWER

I know that this problem does cause many people a lot of heartache. I do believe however that if, or when, the horse works correctly from behind through his back, and accepts the bit, he will want to lower when given a free rein. In the meantime you can assist the process by, first, making him relax when he comes to walk. Avoid any hurrying or tension in yourself. Try squeezing him forward by using your legs asking him to soften in the mouth, using an alternate feel and ease contact on each side. Then offer a lighter rein contact to see whether he will lengthen. He may give a little, in which case repeat the process on the longer rein and try offering again and again until he achieves the lengthening you are looking for.

It may take some time but this 'working down' should succeed if you are patient.

The free walk on a long rein should entail keeping a very light contact. If this is done it will be possible to remind the horse that he can stay stretched, using the above method, until it is time to bring him together.

Question
I am told that my collected walk is irregular. What can I do about it?

ANSWER
Difficulties often occur when collection is required. This is due to a discrepancy in the true acceptance of the aids, either by legs or hands or both.

This discrepancy manifests itself in resistance in the mouth, poll or back of the horse. Any resistance causes muscle 'blockage' which can result in uneven steps. This can be in front or behind, one foot taking a shorter stride than the other, and would be described as irregular.

There are at least two other possibilities. Some horses will show resistance to collection by lifting their front feet higher than their back feet, giving an appearance of the Spanish Walk. This can be overcome by riding forwards and achieving better acceptance of the bit.

An even more unpleasant resistance, in my opinion, is an untrue walk sequence, i.e. pacing: a lateral gait where the feet on the same side come forward together instead of separately. It can be quite difficult to correct but is generally associated with too much speed and tension.

Half halts applied to reduce speed and a calming influence by the rider should aid relaxation and bring about a truer walk.

Question
In extended walk I am uncertain how much rein to give. Can you help?

ANSWER

In the extended walk the horse should walk out to his maximum ability, his hind feet overtracking the print of the forefeet. To achieve this he needs to stretch his head and neck forward, the nose being slightly in front of the vertical, which he can do only if he is allowed to have his neck lower than he would for medium or collected walk, but not lower than a horizontal line from the withers. You should give sufficient rein to allow all this to happen whilst maintaining a light contact with the horse's mouth.

Normally a stretching forward of the rider's arm will give the leeway required, and make it unnecessary to actually lengthen the reins.

Question

I have a lot of trouble with tension in extended walk and a tendency to 'break'; any ideas?

ANSWER

I know this is a difficult problem if you have the sort of horse who is always on the go, or perhaps is always anticipating the following movement. One thing you can do is to make sure that you are not tense yourself and that your seat and thigh muscles are relaxed. Although it would not be acceptable in an advanced test, in lower standard tests a small reassuring stroke on the neck with one hand may be useful. Also, make sure that during training at home you do not always immediately trot or canter after an extended walk, try practising extended walk, walk on a loose rein, extended walk and so on, so that the horse does not anticipate so much.

Question

In the walk pirouette my horse's hind legs always seem to get stuck so that he swivels round. Could you give me advice on how to correct this?

ANSWER

The first thing to do is to decide what the walk is like coming into the half pirouette. It needs to be very active and collected so that the steps are shortened and heightened. Make your pirouette bigger; if the hind legs are swivelling, the walk has actually stopped, so think of keeping up the impulsion and then try to make the hind legs describe a small half circle.

It may help to think of doing a half pass with the quarters in so that the whole horse comes round the pirouette, curved in the direction in which he is going, stepping forwards and coming round at the same time.

When you have mobility of the hind feet, try reducing the size of the pirouette until you are marking time behind. If it goes wrong again, go forwards and try again.

Do remember the importance of using the inside leg to keep up the impulsion, but beware also of muddling the horse by pushing him away from it because this would totally contradict the outside leg which is preventing the quarters from swinging out.

Question

My horse's trot has been described as 'flat'. What does this mean and is there anything I can do?

ANSWER

Horses can vary a lot in the quality of their trot and in the amount of spring they have in their stride.

If you can visualise the way the legs move in trot you can probably appreciate how the trot could be described as flat. The legs move diagonally, each pair coming to the ground alternately, i.e. near fore, off hind; off fore, near hind. As each pair leaves the ground there should be a moment of suspension. Some horses will, naturally, show this clearly and others less so. If the horse does not naturally have this moment of suspension, the rider has to endeavour to create one.

Developing a good regular stride in a steady rhythm helps to produce this, but it is not possible without energy (impulsion) and the activity of the hind legs; the hind legs must move under the horse enabling him to 'lift' himself.

Some trots can be difficult to improve but most will do so by gradual building up of impulsion and collection.

Question

I have always understood that a horse should have good suspension in trot which my horse has naturally, but I seem to be losing marks constantly in competition for being too elevated. Is this so wrong?

ANSWER

You are certainly correct in that a horse should show a moment of suspension between one diagonal and the other, and you are fortunate if your horse has this naturally.

There are, however, things which can go wrong. I suspect that your horse is not going forward with sufficient energy. He may be using his natural elevation as an evasion to working really hard enough. His elevation must be combined with impulsion to take him forwards, not simply upwards.

When you trot your horse try to assess whether he is covering ground, getting where he is going energetically, or whether the whole thing feels as if it is in slow motion. Too much elevation at a slow speed will be like a low passage and would certainly lose marks.

For a time you may have to try to increase the tempo to get him out of this habit. Riding forwards more energetically will gradually achieve this.

When you work on collection you may come up against the same problem again, but using variation within the gait (i.e. lengthening and shortening the stride) and transitions, with a firm seat and leg to keep him forward to the hand, will help.

Question
I am told that I should have my horse regular in trot. I am not really sure what this means.

ANSWER
The word regular is used to describe steps which are rhythmic.

In dressage competitions one of the main requirements is that a horse should show good regular (rhythmic) gaits. It is only possible to achieve regularity, if the speed (tempo) of the steps is steady. If there is rushing due to tension, lack of balance, etc. the speed will vary as will the rhythm (regularity).

One of the first things to do in training is to establish a speed at which the horse can work in balance, so that a rhythm can develop. Obviously a good deal depends on the rider's feel and ability to keep his horse's gaits regular.

Question
When do I start teaching my horse to do lengthened trot?

ANSWER
I think that there may be some variance of opinion as to whether the stride should be lengthened before or after teaching the horse some collection. It may also depend on the horse's stride.

There are, however, several factors which are important in any case.

Firstly, the balance of the horse in trot should be established sufficiently so that if any change in the gait is asked for he does not immediately tip onto the forehand.

Secondly, it is important that the horse should be straight and therefore very even in the stride. Any crookedness will cause unlevel steps which is not only incorrect, but will also make it more difficult for the horse to comply with the rider's aids.

Thirdly, the horse will not lengthen his trot easily if he is insufficiently on the aids.

Finally, unless the hind legs are working under the horse, he will be unable to lengthen satisfactorily.

I believe, therefore, that an element of collection resulting from the use of the half halt to bring the horse together, is really necessary before attempting lengthening.

Question

I am not clear how I should achieve extensions in the various gaits. How is this done?

ANSWER

All extensions rely on a build up of energy and balance. This build up is based on the ability to make a variation within the gait, in a small way at first, using half halts, the horse responding instantly to being brought together, or sent forwards.

When this small variation is achieved smoothly, without resistance, and maintaining a regular rhythmic stride, the horse is prepared for a greater lengthening of the stride.

Greater controlled impulsion, plus the ability to collect, will gradually enable the horse to produce a longer stride in the same rhythm, without losing balance. If the horse falls onto his forehand he will be unable to produce a longer stride. Similarly, if he fails to respond to the leg aids, or leans against the hand, he will not be in a position to respond sufficiently.

Question

Whenever I try to ride a serpentine in trot my horse puts his head up in the middle of it and is marked down in competitions. Can you tell me why he does this?

ANSWER

Generally speaking, horses alter the position of their head

and neck to save their balance.

In this case I would guess that your horse is more stiff on one side than the other and is failing to give an equal bend in each direction. To make it easier for himself he alters his head position. I think you should go back to circles for a time and make sure that he answers your inside leg.

The shoulder-in exercise is invaluable for gaining better control of bend.

Question
When I am cantering, every time I want to circle, and quite often in the corners, he changes legs behind and becomes disunited. How can I prevent this happening?

ANSWER
The reason your horse changes leg behind is partly lack of balance but mostly stiffness. He is resisting the bend you require for the start of a circle or coming into a corner.

You can help him by making him more supple in walk and trot, really making him bend round your inside leg, using circles of varying sizes and the shoulder-in exercise. This should also help to improve his ability to answer your aids in the canter as well, and make him more balanced. Do make sure that he is listening to both leg aids: the inside one sending him forward, and the outside one keeping the quarters round the inside leg.

When you come to canter again the situation should be better but if it is still not satisfactory, use your outside leg and outside rein together. This temporarily removes the bend, but he will not be able to change legs behind if there is sufficient control from the outside hand. You will gradually be able to retake the bend.

Question
When I give my aids for canter or if I want to go more forwards in canter, my horse sometimes humps his back. What is he doing and why?

ANSWER

First of all check that there is nothing wrong with your horse's back. Make sure that the saddle is not rubbing him and making him sore, and that it is not pinching him. If all is well then the answer is that the horse is resisting the leg aids. A form of napping.

He has discovered that if he humps his back, he can push your seat out of the saddle. This reduces its effectiveness, allowing him to do his own thing and work far less hard than he should. For a time he will probably need the use of the schooling whip to reinforce the leg aids. If he gets a sharp smack he will realise that his little game is not on!

Send him forwards strongly from seat and leg every time he humps his back so that you have more impulsion. When you control this energy make sure that you keep him well forwards to the hand, and do not let him drop behind the leg, or come off the bit.

Use plenty of variations within the gait and be determined!

Question

My horse won't strike off on the left leg in canter. What do I do?

ANSWER

Persistent difficulty in obtaining the correct lead in canter can be particularly tiresome for the novice rider. Experience generally overcomes this problem quite quickly because the horse usually strikes off correctly if put in the right position. Less knowledgeable riders find it difficult to feel this positioning. There are several ways to try to overcome the problem.

A horse will strike off more readily on the inside lead if he is asked for it in a corner of the school, or on a circle. Try to achieve a fairly active trot initially with the horse going forwards well into the bridle. He should be as balanced as possible.

If he will not answer the correct aids, i.e. inside leg on the girth, outside leg behind the girth, inside rein asking a very small flexion, outside rein controlling the speed and size of the circle or corner, then the use of the schooling whip behind the outside leg should be employed. A sharp tap with the schooling whip and a strong aid from the inside leg should help the strike off.

However, if the horse has seldom cantered on the correct leg, either because he is stubborn, or because he has never been made to do so, it may be necessary to make him take outside bend into the strike off. The rider will take a strong flexion to the outside of the circle or corner, away from the leg upon which he wants the the horse to lead. This will have the effect of putting extra weight onto the outside shoulder, freeing the inside leg. To save his balance the horse may strike off correctly.

If the correct lead is obtained it is important to keep the canter going, for one or two circuits of the school or field, to give the horse the idea that he can canter on that leg.

Another horse positioned in the centre of the circle may encourage some horses to strike off correctly. In extreme cases a pole or cavalletti placed on the track in a corner of the school will sometimes do the trick. Trot the horse over it and push on as you get there. The horse will probably partly jump which will cause him to canter and I have found that in most cases he will land on the inside lead.

It is important to recognise when the correct lead is achieved because if the rider fails to push on quickly, the horse may fall back to trot and will not learn what he is meant to do.

Question
How can I stop my horse putting his head up going into canter?

ANSWER

This is very common problem and often tiresome to correct.

Theoretically, the answer is to make the horse more obedient to the aids; practically, it can be hard to achieve. I believe that the horse does this to help lift himself into canter, but if this is necessary it does indicate insufficient energy driving him into that gait.

I have found that increasing the energy in the trot and containing it in the hand, certainly helps. This, with an increased action of the squeezing of the fingers prevents the mouth setting at the moment of strike-off. If the horse (and rider) understands a shoulder-in position, this is very helpful in overcoming this problem.

Shoulder-in at walk or trot should be taken on the long side. Coming into a corner reduce the angle, but keep the aids on and then ask at once for the canter. This is also very useful for horses who are difficult about a certain leg.

Question

I constantly have trouble in canter with my horse carrying his quarters in. I have tried to push them out but it seems to make matters worse. What can I do?

ANSWER

Any attempt at pushing out quarters which are carried in from the track will certainly be ineffective. The correction should be made to the forehand by taking a shoulder-in position. It may be necessary to first effect some straightening of the horse's neck because it will almost certainly be curled inwards as well. This should be done by using more outside rein into the neck, not only to straighten the neck, but to prevent too much weight being carried on the outside shoulder.

If the shoulder-in can be performed satisfactorily in trot, the horse will know the aids, and it should be possible to use these aids to obtain a shoulder-in position in canter.

Once the forehand has been positioned, the quarters will

sort themselves out and begin to follow the forehand correctly.

Question
I am trying to teach my horse counter canter, but find that he keeps changing legs in front. What can I do to prevent this?

ANSWER
Your horse is changing legs and becoming disunited because he is lacking in balance.

Try riding a very shallow loop on the long side of the school, with only a small gradual deviation from the track. Make sure you start the loop at the first quarter marker after the short side, come off the track a little, run parallel to it for a few strides and then gradually take him back to the track at the quarter marker at the end of the long side.

Although the flexion should be maintained to the leading leg, avoid too much bend until the horse has learned the exercise. Keep him as equal to both hands and legs as you can, but try to give more support to the shoulder opposite to the leading leg by keeping that rein well in to the neck.

Your outside leg should be a little further back than usual to keep him to the leading leg. You will need more push during your loop to keep the impulsion.

Do also make sure that you have a steady enough canter to be able to ask for counter lead because if there is too much speed the horse will lose his balance and change legs whatever you do.

Question
In my canter pirouette I find that I lose control and the horse seems to get round quicker than I do! What is wrong?

ANSWER
Your horse is being over helpful! He obviously knows the

exercise and as soon as he feels you tell him to start, decides to get it over as quickly as possible. There must be a certain amount of tension, I imagine, for this to arise because speed is often connected to anxiety. You should check on two points to begin with. Make sure that the horse is calm in his canter and rounded in his outline and that he will let you position him in canter, i.e. a very slight shoulder-in position. He must do this without getting steamed up.

Question

I have been trying to teach my horse to do canter pirouettes but he lifts very high in front and seems to move in slow motion. Can you suggest what I might do?

ANSWER

The most important factor in the canter pirouette is to actually keep the canter! This is not meant to be a facetious remark; it is the difficult part of the exercise.

If the canter is true and short (collected) enough, the coming round is no problem. If your horse is tending to lift his forehand to get round, basically he has a lack of impulsion. He is trying to comply with the aids, labouring in the process, but his hind legs are getting stuck to the spot as he heaves his forehand round.

I would suggest a rethink on your collected canter. Is it really collected enough and does the horse stay round in his outline? Can he do an almost on-the-spot canter for a few strides at a time in the same tempo? If the tempo is slowing then he needs more leg from the rider creating energy to keep the activity.

I suggest that you ride the pirouette more forward and make it bigger until you can come round in a true canter, keeping him rounded with the correct tempo and bend.

Question

My canter pirouette is sometimes described by dressage

judges as a 'turn on the centre'. Can you explain exactly what this means and what I should do?

ANSWER

In a canter pirouette the hind feet describe a very small circle almost on the spot, and the forehand makes a bigger circle. This is achieved by the rider controlling the hindquarters with the inside leg on the girth to keep the canter, and the outside leg behind the girth to prevent the quarters swinging out. The hands are bringing the forehand round by the use of the inside rein to flex the horse in the direction he is going, and the outside rein controlling speed, collection and the size of the stride as it comes round.

In a full pirouette, approximately eight strides would complete the exercise. Because it is hard work, the horse may evade the proper use of the pirouette in which the horse must lower the hindquarters and bring the hind legs further under his body to support his forehand. He will evade in various ways but one way is to try to swing his quarters out against the rider's outside leg. In this way he will avoid 'sitting', when he would have to flex his joints more, and gets away with a stiff back and an incorrect exercise.

In this case the forehand may eventually come round to the new direction, but the quarters will not have described a smaller circle. This is often called a turn on the centre.

A good exercise for correcting this evasion is to canter a small circle. Start with a 10 m circle and position the quarters in. When the horse is attending better to the rider's outside leg, the size of the circle can gradually be reduced until a pirouette is achieved.

At all times it should be possible to bring the horse back onto a true circle if desired.

In the build up to the full pirouette, alternate use of quarters-in and shoulder-in position may help the rider to obtain better control.

Question

In the canter half pass I find it very difficult to get any bend. Could you advise me?

ANSWER

There are several factors to consider.

First of all, think about the sort of canter you have. Is it collected enough? Does it have enough impulsion? It will be very difficult for your horse to give the bend you need if he is strung out or lacking in energy.

Can you ride a circle of 8 m or 10 m with a good bend? This is the sort of curve that the horse will need to make in the half pass. You will have to be able to make him curve round your inside leg from the use of your outside leg and be able to take a shoulder-in position with the forehand.

He will need to be very responsive to your inside leg because it is this leg which will be responsible for maintaining, or increasing if necessary, the energy and the bend. It is this leg too, which must also maintain the lift of the canter because, if this is lost, the horse will not be able to gain ground in the moment of suspension. Additionally, the inside leg must prevent the horse falling onto his inside shoulder which will certainly cause loss of bend. Its correct use will keep the canter upright and forward to the hand enabling the rider to shape the bend of the forehand.

Question

How much bend should I have in the half pass? I am always being told by judges that I have too little.

ANSWER

The amount of bend required in the half pass is determined by the angle. For example if the arena is 20 by 60 metres and the half pass is from D to M the angle will be less than if the half pass is from D to B. A bend should be taken uniformly through the horse with his face looking towards the marker, his shoulders positioned towards the marker and his hindquarters made to come round the inside leg of the rider.

Question
Could you explain the aids for a flying change?

ANSWER
The aids are exactly the same as for canter, i.e. inside leg on the girth, used to send the horse forwards, outside leg behind the girth to tell him which leg to canter on, inside rein used for flexion to leading leg, outside rein used for control. The difference being that the horse maintains canter, the change occurring in the moment of suspension.

Changes are achieved by establishing a balanced canter in a round outline with well-controlled impulsion. If the horse responds to the canter aids as he feels them being altered, and providing he is kept in canter he will gradually learn what is wanted. Initial use of the schooling whip may be needed to stress the leg aids but on no account upset the horse.

Some horses will take longer than others to grasp what is being asked. Care should be taken to use consistant aids and remain in a secure position in the saddle.

Question
How do I correct 'swinging' flying changes?

ANSWER
Whenever there is a crookedness in training, the solution is to ride the horse more forward.

Swinging changes are generally caused by a crookedness in the canter. This is most likely to be on the side to which the horse prefers to hollow himself. Most horses try to do this but more expert riders will prevent it happening.

For example, on the right rein the horse will bend his neck too much to the inside and also try to carry his quarters to the right. In the flying change from the left to the right he will adopt this quarters-in position as he changes, which will cause a swing. He may also try to jump to the right, making it impossible to keep a straight line. As with any crookedness in the canter the correction is made to the forehand, not directly to the quarters.

If a shoulder-in position is taken, together with a stronger inside leg to send the horse more forward, a straightening is effected. This method is carried through the changes and, although resistances may be encountered to start with, the horse will gradually allow himself to be made straighter and more controlled.

Question
My horse keeps being 'late behind' in his flying changes. What can I do about this?

ANSWER
I think that this fault, like most faults in the flying change, depends very much on the quality of the canter itself.

Basically, the canter must be going forwards with plenty of impulsion so that there is a good moment of suspension. This is important because that moment of suspension is when the flying change occurs, so if it is too flat there will be no room for the change to be made.

Impulsion is important to the collection of the horse and ensures that he is not on his forehand. Late changes often occur because there is too much weight on the horse's shoulders. This gives the quarters too much opportunity to become raised, enabling the horse to make short or late changes with a hind leg.

As with all exercises, the better the horse accepts the aids, the better the chance of correct changes. The rider must be very clear with his aids and well co-ordinated.

The rider's inside leg will be of particular importance in obtaining the flying change because its positive use will send the horse forward and obtain the new bend. The effective action of this inside leg will certainly help to reduce the chance of late changes.

Late changes also happen very often because the rider has either failed to change the bend as the aid is given with the legs, or because the horse resists the change of bend and falls onto his inside shoulder. If this is happening, try changing the flexion a little before the leg aids so that the horse is more prepared and partly in position.

Question
What is the difference between tempi and sequence flying changes?

ANSWER
None, they mean the same thing.

Question
How do I teach my horse to stand square?

ANSWER
Some horses bring themselves to a square halt naturally, and others persistently do not. It is the acceptance of the aids coming into halt that helps initially.

In the early stages with novice or young horses, it may be wise to accept a straight halt, even if it is not quite square. If the horse is calm, correction may be attempted by the rider using the legs to bring the horse together more. If this does not work, a schooling whip may be used very lightly on the offending leg.

Praise must be given for a correct response. An assistant on the ground could use a whip lightly on any leg left behind, to aid the rider.

Also, as a matter of discipline, always try to make your horse stand square for mounting, grooming and on the lunge. It will then become a matter of habit and be easier to achieve when ridden.

Question
My horse won't stand still. How do I make him?

ANSWER

Horses vary in the ways in which they will not stand still. Some are merely ignorant or not very bright, wandering or moving about at will, unless the rider is really firm. Young horses may not understand what is being required of them. Nervous horses can be worried by being made to stand because they tend to feel 'trapped' by the aids. Some may be anxious because they have been made to square up, and keep moving a foot hoping that this is what is wanted. Whatever the reason, better use of aids should help.

When your horse really accepts the legs and the bit, he can be brought to a halt under control. A pat or praising by the voice should soothe the anxious horse, and, in time, the less bright horse will realise that he is required to stand still. Do be careful not to hang on to the horse's mouth in halt because this will make him want to evade the hands. It is also a mistake to take your legs away from his sides because then there is nothing to hold the horse forward to the hands, or to control the quarters.

Calmness is essential in achieving a good halt and firm aids and repetition should help.

Question
How and when do I start teaching collection?

ANSWER
The horse should be going well forwards from the legs and be submissive to the bit. He should be straight, balanced and holding a steady regular stride, and should be able to do half halts. He would then be sufficiently prepared to learn to shorten his steps, which is achieved by the use of the half halt. The shortening may be sustained for a few strides so that the horse learns to rebalance. He will try to vary the impulsion but it should be kept forward to the hand, aided by the schooling whip if necessary. He may come heavy in the hand to begin with, but as he finds his balance he should be able to lighten.

The rider must keep the horse straight and ride energetically but smoothly forward after the shortening. This process is repeated over a period of days or weeks until the horse can hold the shorter strides for himself.

Gradually, more impulsion is asked for to enable the horse to become more compressed; he can then be asked to sustain the collection over longer periods.

Question
How do I know if I have got my horse collected?

ANSWER
There is quite a positive difference when you have got it right. The hind legs feel further under the horse's body and the hindquarters are full of energy. The steps feel more springy and 'off the ground'. The back feels spongelike to sit on. The forehand feels higher with the neck arching up in front. The head is more bent at the poll, the nose further in towards a vertical position with the mouth 'giving' to the hands. The movements all seem easier to ride.

It is possible to be misled by the steps being shorter but not higher owing to a lack of impulsion. The horse may also feel compressed, but only because he has drawn back in his neck, and not because he is using his quarters.

He may be shortening, but he will be hollow in the back instead of round, which will give the feeling of sitting in a dish. The back will probably be hard instead of soft.

In collection the hind feet should not come into the print which the forefeet leave because the impulsion gives more elevation to the steps.

Question
Can you explain the difference between impulsion and activity, or are they the same thing?

ANSWER

I think that, to most people, impulsion means the energy in the hindquarters which takes the horse forward. Activity is the effort which the hind legs make in respect of flexion of the joints, which give lift to the stride.

Some horses are very active behind but do not go forwards as well, and some are driving themselves along but with very little flexion of the joints.

Question

I am always being told I should use more half halts in training, but I don't think I really understand what they are. Could you enlighten me?

ANSWER

Half halts are invaluable during training for many reasons. They, basically, help to balance the horse which is essential to correct work. They are used to steady excitable horses, to engage lazy horses, to bring about collection, and to prepare for many exercises.

Before you can ride a half halt, it is necessary to be able to ride correct transitions with the horse remaining on the aids. He must allow himself to be ridden forward from the seat and leg into the bridle without resistance, accepting the bringing together of the hindquarters and the forehand. When this is performed with ease, then the half halt or semi-transition may be introduced.

Think of it as almost a transition to the next gait, but not quite; a kind of 'pause', but without loss of impulsion. It is only momentary and it is very important that the horse goes forward immediately following. Bear in mind that the purpose of the half halt is to balance or rebalance the horse, so in riding forward after it, do not then push him back onto his forehand or out of the rhythm.

Half halts may be used in varying degrees. With a young or novice horse the degree of half halt is little more than a steadying aid. As the horse learns to accept collecting aids the degree increases.

Most half halts fail because riders do not use the leg aids sufficiently, so do bear this in mind.

Question
My horse will not bend to the left, what shall I do?

ANSWER
If your horse has difficulty in giving a bend to the left, it is probably because he has been allowed to keep his head to the right most of the time.

The muscles on the right-hand side of his neck will therefore be contracted, so when you try to take a left bend, the shortened muscles prevent him from doing so. Your first aim should be to get him straight by riding him with more even contact from leg and hand. When he is straighter then ask for a small flexion to the left and, gradually, over a period of time, ask for more.

Circles and shoulder-in on both reins will help to make his muscles more even.

Question
My horse is on the forehand. How do I stop this happening?

ANSWER
The reason he is on the forehand is that his balance is incorrect. His weight should be carried more equally over his four legs, with a gradual transfer to the hindquarters as training progresses.

The exercises which will help this transfer are transitions and half halts. These need to be ridden properly, of course. Improvement will only be achieved by using the legs to encourage more energy from behind, which will then be controlled and contained by the hands.

Providing there is no resistance to these aids, the hind legs will come further under the body, improving distribution of weight, thus lightening the forehand.

Question
Does the turn on the forehand have any real use in training. If so, when would it be used?

ANSWER
I believe that the main purpose for teaching the horse this exercise is primarily to teach him to yield to the pressure of the rider's inside leg, for the purpose of being able to move the hindquarters away from any object. It would normally be taught early in the young horse's training.

At one time it was thought that as the hindquarters moved round, the horse should be expected to pivot on his inside foreleg. However, nowadays this is not a criterion, the importance being laid upon the response the horse makes to the rider's leg aids.

Question
I do seem to have a lot of trouble keeping straight on a centre line. Can you help at all?

ANSWER
In walk and trot it is only possible to keep straight if the horse is equally responsive to both legs and on both sides of his mouth, and if he is equally supple.

In canter you should be able to take a shoulder-in position to the leading leg in order to control the forehand. If the forehand is kept controlled, the quarters will be unable to wander and will follow the front.

In walk and trot, the rider should see the C marker between the horse's ears as he comes up the centre.

In canter and, indeed, at all times on the centre line, the rider must keep his eye on the C or A markers, depending on which way he is going, and immediately correct any slight deviation.

I think it is almost impossible to ride straight at any gait unless the horse knows the shoulder-in exercise, so that the forehand can be corrected. Any attempt to straighten the quarters without this control will only produce more swinging.

Question

I seem to be losing a lot of marks in transitions because my horse is 'not forward'. Could you explain what this means?

ANSWER

So often in transitions the rider uses the reins to slow the horse without sufficient support from the legs. This has the effect of stopping the impulsion, that energy which is taking the horse forward to the next gait. For a moment, or even a few steps, that energy is lost or delayed which affects the following movement and probably allows the horse to fall on his forehand, lean on the hand, resist the bit and so on.

Although we are taught to use our legs, many riders are unaware of the extent to which this is necessary to keep the engagement of the hindquarters. In all transitions up and particularly down, firm use of a deep seat and strong legs will help to keep the horse forward and balanced.

Question

In circles I am continually losing marks in competitions for not having a 'true bend'. I do not understand what this means. Could you explain?

ANSWER

There could be several reasons why you are losing marks.

Horses which are stiff evade in quite a few ways. For instance, your horse could be tilting his head, crossing his jaw, leaning in, putting his hindquarters in, or escaping the bend by curling his neck round to the inside. This would also enable the outside shoulder to take too much weight allowing a drift away from the true curve.

Try riding a few 20 m circles and assess which of these faults you have.

Whatever the fault, the correct bend will only be improved by better acceptance of the aids.

In the case of tilting or crossing the jaw, it will be necessary to check on the acceptance of the bit and see that the horse does so equally on both sides of the mouth.

If the neck is curling round too much, ride the horse straighter and make him listen to your inside leg, which also helps to prevent him leaning in. If the hindquarters are in, you will need to teach him shoulder-in to gain better control of his length. This will also correct any drifting away from the circle.

With circles of any size you must be sure of how to ride them and think of the shoulder-in aids.

Question

My horse puts his head up in rein-back and goes rigid, refusing to go back. What can I do?

ANSWER

A horse can only rein-back if his back is rounded, not hollow, and if he is correctly on the aids. If he is getting his head up he is escaping the aids, inevitably becoming hollow in his back, resulting in tense muscles which become painful if force is employed.

I think you should practise some transitions from walk to halt to walk and so on until you are quite certain that you can keep him on the aids and in a rounded shape throughout those exercises. Do be sure to use your legs and keep them on the whole time including during the pause of the halt.

When this seems satisfactory try the rein-back from the halt using the legs, not too strongly, into a resisting hand. If the horse makes a step back remaining on the aids, pat him and walk on, repeating this and gradually increasing the number of steps back.

51

I think it important that the hand should ease between the steps to begin with because slow deliberate steps are much more controllable and you do not want the horse to rush backwards.

If you still find you are having problems getting the horse to understand, try to get someone to help from the ground using a whip gently on each of the forelegs in turn, using your aids at the same time.

If you have taught the horse to step backwards in the stable using your voice, try this use of voice while mounted.

If he still tries to put his head up, ride forwards each time and correct him. I am sure patience will win through eventually.

Question
My horse's head always seems to be moving up and down. Why is this?

ANSWER
Unsteady head carriage is generally caused by the rider failing to keep a consistent or firm contact.

A firm contact can only be taken and maintained as the result of energy being created by the rider's legs to make the horse go forwards into the bridle.

This energy is then controlled by the use of the reins. If the rider's contact is variable, the horse's mouth will receive intermittent messages, instead of a steady one. This will cause him to move his head, either fairly passively up and down, or possibly more violently as he get fed up with the discomfort in his mouth.

Question
When I ask my horse to come on the bit he puts his head in the air? What can I do?

ANSWER

The most important thing to do is to persevere and not be put off by the difficulty. Also, as with all aids, do have a think about the way you are asking him to come onto the bit.

He must first respond to the legs, listening to them in halt, and going forward from them as requested. Then he must be asked to soften in the mouth by a squeezing action of the fingers, probably used alternately, or held firmly on the softer side and squeezed more firmly on the harder side.

Some horses can be very stubborn about yielding to the aids, but persistence on the part of the rider can overcome the problem.

Question

I have been told that because my horse is an Arab I cannot make him go on the bit, is this true?

ANSWER

Any horse of any breeding can be trained to go on the bit. It is all a matter of asking in the right way. Arabs have a reputation for being independant creatures who prefer to do their own thing. This is nonsense, very probably it is the owners who want to do their own thing and are not prepared to put in the work to teach their horses to come on the bit.

Question

I am having trouble keeping the angle in my shoulder-in. Can you help?

ANSWER

The answer lies in discovering whether you really have the horse accepting the inside leg and the outside rein, and whether the horse is sufficiently collected. If he is truly answering the aids and is gathered together, it will be possible to control the angle.

Most mistakes occur owing to the rider trying to achieve the angle by using too much inside rein. This has the effect of bending the neck, rather than bringing the horse's shoulders off the track. A slack outside rein will allow the horse's shoulders to fall back into the track, and will make it impossible to keep the position. Failure to respond adequately to the rider's inside leg will cause loss of impulsion. This will prevent the horse's inside hind leg from coming up under his body, which it must do if he is to be able to carry himself in a shoulder-in position.

The rider's outside leg must assist the exercise by controlling the hindquarters. If they swing out the horse's bend will be lost, in which case the exercise will end up as a leg yield, not a shoulder-in. The angle may also be changed if the collection is unsatisfactory.

If the horse is not gathered together well he will labour because he is too spread out and be unable to do the exercise correctly.

Speed may also cause difficulties. If the steps are too quick and not keeping to a regular rhythm, the horse will run onto his outside shoulder thus losing his position.

Question
Do I need to teach my horse to leg yield before teaching him other lateral movements?

ANSWER
I think it can be quite an advantage to teach leg yielding to a novice horse, particularly for less experienced riders. It does give both horse and rider the idea of going away from the leg. More experienced riders will use a yield from the inside leg sometimes in corners or on a circle.

It is not essential to teach leg yielding before teaching other lateral movements providing the rider has knowledge of those movements.

I believe the horse should be kept quite straight when leg

yielding so that there is no risk of the outside shoulder escaping.

Question
I always seem to lose the bend in a half pass. What am I doing wrong?

ANSWER
Successful half passes depend on several points.

The half pass cannot succeed unless there is sufficient impulsion coming forward to the hand. This impulsion must be created by the use of the rider's inside leg. There also has to be sufficient bend.

The bend is formed by the use of shoulder-in to put the shoulders in a position where they can take the horse forwards and across to where he is going. In order to be able to hold the bend and position, the horse will need to be collected.

The collection is achieved by the use of half halts which keep the stride short enough to enable the horse to move across laterally. The hindquarters will be required to come further round the rider's inside leg to make the bend, therefore the horse must be responsive to the outside leg aid.

If all these points are satisfactory, half pass should be possible.

There are, however, a few additional points which might be helpful.

Before even beginning to try a half pass, try riding a route from the centre line to the side line with a good flexion to the side you want the bend i.e. in a 40 m × 20 m area on the right rein, turn up the centre line. At D turn right towards M. Flex head, and neck a little, to right. Do not allow shoulders to deviate from that line. Practise this several times on both reins.

Progress by coming up the centre line and commencing two or three steps of shoulder-in (in canter shoulder-in position). Keeping the bend, position the shoulders towards the M marker and ride firmly forwards with the inside leg. If the bend is lost ride into shoulder-in again (in canter shoulder-in position) then try the half pass again. (In canter it is not possible to achieve the same shoulder-in angle as in trot, but a lesser degree of the exercise is possible. This is called shoulder-in position, rather than shoulder-in.)

Most mistakes are made by riders trying to push their horse across from the outside leg without putting the shoulders round towards the marker to which they are going. This causes dropping of impulsion and resistance because the angle is too difficult.

Riders often find the co-ordination of this exercise very difficult. Try thinking of bend aids for a circle. It is not quite that simple, but it may help.

Question
I have taught my horse shoulder-in and half pass. Are there any other lateral movements which I should use?

ANSWER
There are two other lateral exercises related to the half pass, which are the travers (half pass head to wall) and renvers (half pass tail to wall).

Both these movements would hold the same principles regarding aids, bend, collection, impulsion and so on, as the half pass, performed at an angle of 30 degrees to the wall or centre line.

There are also counter changes of hand, or zig zag, either in trot or canter.

The main points to look for are equal bend to each direction, the correct number of steps, if specified, and correct changes if performed in canter.

Question

In the counter changes of hand, I find that I continually get the quarters leading. Also, I can't seem to get in the number specified in the test I am trying to do. Can you help at all?

ANSWER
The answer to your problem regarding quarters leading in any of the lateral work is to correct the forehand.

If you take a slight shoulder-in position prior to your sideways movement, this will put the forehand a little ahead of the quarters. Then, if the horse bends round your inside leg, the angle of the lateral exercise will be correct.

Similarly during a counter change of hand, it will be necessary to put the forehand into shoulder-in position before asking the quarters to change direction.

Alternatively, it may help to finish one direction of the half pass and then take a renvers position prior to the new direction. This will also put the shoulders into position, and keep the hindquarters under control, then all you have to do is to change the bend.

I expect that the reason you cannot get in the number of counter changes that you want is because the horse is lacking collection. You will need to improve the collection before trying to fit in more changes of direction.

Question
I have been trying to teach my horse to piaffe but I am told he is doing passage steps. What does this mean and how can I stop him?

ANSWER
If this is happening, there could be two possible reasons:
1. He may be using steps which are too elevated for executing the exercise correctly.
2. You may have obtained too much impulsion too soon before he really knows what is wanted.

Either way he must be got out of this quickly before it becomes too established because it can become quite difficult to correct.

I do not know, of course, how you have been trying to teach your horse the piaffe. If you are teaching him mounted, as opposed to from the ground, you will need to make him more forward-going to avoid the lifting steps of the passage. To achieve this, try using transitions from trot to halt to trot, with only a brief pause for the halt.

When he is doing these transitions obediently with no resistances, try shortening the steps before and after the halt, but keeping the horse well in front of the leg. If he tries to drop the bit or hollow his back, ride forward energetically and then try again.

The steps out of the halt will gradually become shorter teaching the horse to lower his quarters, helping him to stay closer to the ground in the correct tempo.

Question
In the piaffe I am told that my horse is stepping back with one front leg. What is causing this and what do I do?

ANSWER
Because the piaffe is a highly collected trot on the spot, the sequence of legs would be diagonal, i.e. one foreleg with the opposite hind leg coming to the ground together, with a small moment of suspension followed by the other fore and hind leg together.

You are encountering either a dropping of impulsion or more probably a resistance on one side of the horse's mouth which prevents the impulsion going through the horse.

If you feel that you are losing impulsion then clearly you need to activate the hindquarters more and get the horse to go forwards. The collection and shortening of the steps must be in your control not the idea of the horse.

If you think that there is a resistance in the mouth or if the horse will not stay straight, you may need to defer your piaffe attempts until the horse is more satisfactorily supple. Use lateral exercises and flexions to improve suppleness. Whatever the cause, stepping back should be corrected by riding forwards strongly before it becomes a habit. When you return to the piaffe again try to approach it more progressively.

Question
Could you tell me how to begin to teach passage?

ANSWER
If the piaffe and the transition from piaffe to trot is well under control, you may be ready to begin passage.

It will be important to have a very regular, collected trot, without resistance, well forward and on the aids. As the impulsion is increased it will be necessary to use the half halt frequently so this exercise must be well established.

Only from the combination of the impulsion and the half-halt will you start to achieve elevation which will only be for a step or two at first. You should then ride firmly forward in trot, making sure that rhythm is maintained. If you have difficulty in obtaining impulsion, an assistant on the ground may be able to help, but it is unwise to use someone with insufficient knowledge of the required rhythm and height.

Do make sure from the start that both hind legs work independently and evenly both in length of stride and activity. If you are doubtful at all, it would be best to get professional help.

It is always difficult to eradicate things that have gone wrong.

Question
I would like to teach my horse to passage, but do I have to do piaffe first?

ANSWER
You should try to establish piaffe first. If you do it the other way round, then when you do come to piaffe the horse may

try to use his passage steps, which will be too elevated for piaffe and cause considerable difficulty.

It will also probably be simpler to teach him passage from piaffe because this will have put his hindquarters well under him, putting him in a good position for more lift. It will, however, be some time before you can achieve this because the transition from piaffe to trot must be well regulated first.

Question
In the transitions between the piaffe and the passage I seem to lose all impulsion. What am I doing wrong?

ANSWER
I should think that you have tried to go from one to the other too suddenly instead of progressively. The development of these transitions depends on complete acceptance of the half halt, firstly to reduce the size of the steps to piaffe and then to control the size after the piaffe. Perhaps your horse is not yet ready for the precision of this exercise. It demands the highest possible degree of control of every step. He can only do it for you if he is very supple, very energetic and accepting the aids with no resistance.

Question
I am told that my horse is 'nappy'. What exactly does this mean?

ANSWER
It means, basically, that he is doing as he likes, rather than being obedient to your aids.

There are so many ways in which a horse can be nappy, that I can only give a general answer.

Any demand you make of your horse, any movement or exercise you want to do, should be obeyed instantly without resistances of any kind.

If the horse stops and refuses to go forward, kicks out, turns round, bounces on the spot, does not listen to aids etc. then his behaviour constitutes napping.

It can be a big problem if the horse has been nappy for some time because he is going to have to relearn to obey the aids. You may be in for quite a tussle which will involve a lot of determination to win on your part. You are going to have to utilise a whip to overcome the problems because the leg and seat will almost certainly be insufficiently strong.

Try to see it through if you can because a napping horse is unpleasant to ride and, quite often, a danger to himself, his rider and others.

Question
My horse bucks and he often kicks out at the same time. Can you tell me if there is anything I can do to stop him?

ANSWER
It sounds as though he may not be bucking out of sheer high spirits, but as a resistance.

Horses find lots of ways of getting out of what we want them to do and he may have discovered that if he bucks, humps his back or kicks out, he can get you out of the saddle, thus rendering you helpless at that moment.

If he is doing this, it is naughty and disobedient and he should be smacked jolly hard with the whip so that he goes forwards. If it has really become a habit, he may try to carry on bucking or kicking and the only way out of it is to keep using your whip and be more obstinate than he is! It may seem as if he will never give up, but I assure you he will if you are determined.

Bucking from high spirits or because the horse is too fresh is another matter. Try to lunge him for a few minutes before you ride him if you think this is the cause and let him work some energy out of his system.

If he bucks while you are riding, pull his head up and ride him forwards, making him come more securely onto the aids. Then he won't have time to get a buck in!

Question
My horse seems to swish his tail a lot. Is this wrong?

ANSWER
A swishing tail is very often a sign that the horse is not happy in his work, he may be reluctant to do what you want or even nappy.

There are degrees of swishing. An occasional swish may not mean very much, but a lot of activity or angry swishing could certainly be a resistance to the rider's aids. Generally it reflects a dislike of the use of the rider's legs and so it is necessary to teach the horse to accept the leg aids better.

The best way to do this is to give the horse a sharp slap with the whip if he does not answer the legs willingly. As with all training, the improvement may not be immediate but persevere and, given time, it should get better.

Some swishing may be caused by anxiety, so do make sure that all aids are clear, and the exercises are not too complicated for the horse's stage of training.

Question
I have a problem getting my horse past certain objects. They are not always the same things. He just decides not to pass something and will try to turn round. I have tried leading him past and using my stick, but nothing seems to help. Can you suggest anything?

ANSWER
You don't say how old the horse is. Youngsters often do not want to go past new objects which they have not seen before, which is understandable.

It is wise to take an older reliable horse for company who can give a lead, so that this problem does not arise because, unfortunately, once a horse has discovered that he can get away with refusing to pass something, it is quite a nuisance.

Getting off and leading the horse past is really giving in to him. He has been asked to do something and even if he does not fancy the idea, he must learn to do as he is told. If you are alone this can be awkward but a firm line should be taken from the start.

If your horse will not go forwards from the whip and the aids, there is a serious flaw in your training. Horses must be made to respect the whip, in connection with the normal aids, from the beginning. They must be far more worried about upsetting their rider than being concerned about any obstacle they might meet!

Sometimes it may be necessary to sit out a situation rather than entering into a confrontation, which the horse might win. Be prepared to stay all day to win the battle rather than give in otherwise the horse will soon decide that he has the upper hand.

Question

Do you have any suggestions for how to stop spooking? My horse seems to see something where there is nothing.

ANSWER

This can be quite a tiresome problem because undoubtedly there are horses, fortunately in the minority, who do seem to be always looking for trouble. One would imagine them to be of a nervous disposition but this is not necessarily the case. Some of the most laid back horses are the naughtiest. I have found that the only way to overcome their silliness is to be ultra particular regarding obedience. Getting cross is ineffective so, however irritating the horse is, you need to keep calm.

Young horses naturally have some excuse because they will come across many new things which may initially alarm them and they will need reassurance. On the other hand, older horses who persistently spook at things they have seen many times are just being naughty.

One way to prevent the horse from having his own way and make him listen to you is to put him into shoulder-in. This makes it far more difficult for him to escape the aids. As the horse's training advances he will become more obedient and build up trust in his rider, so, although he may try it on sometimes, he will rarely get away with it.

Question
When I am riding, I have noticed that my horse puts his tongue out of the side of his mouth quite a lot. Why does he do it?

ANSWER
This peculiarity is an objection to the presence of the bit. It may originate from an injury to the mouth or tongue, or it could be the result of a severe or badly fitting bit.

The horse may be making himself more comfortable owing to the unsympathetic or restrictive hands of the rider. It can be a very difficult problem to correct because the evasion will become a habit and all habits are hard to cure. Proper use of the aids and improved submission to them will begin to correct the difficulty.

I have found that if the horse is made to go energetically forwards and the mouth kept alive by gentle, but active, action of the fingers, he has less time to think about this evasion.

Question
How can I stop my horse getting his tongue over the bit?

ANSWER
The horse is putting his tongue over the bit because he does not like the pressure of the bit; however, he has to be taught to accept the pressure.

I think there are several things to try. First, fit the bit a little higher in the mouth than you would normally. Make sure it is not too wide because, if it is jointed, the centre will hang down too low and make it easier for the tongue to come over.

Next, use either a drop or flash noseband. This will help to keep the mouth closed making it harder for the horse to get the tongue back. Ride the horse well forward into the hand and keep his mind occupied with responding to the aids.

If the problem persists you could try using a tongue layer, but quite often the horse reverts to the evasion as soon as it is removed.

As a precaution it might be wise to have the horse's mouth checked over by the veterinary surgeon in case there is a physical problem.

Question

I constantly lose marks in dressage competitions because my horse comes above the bit, I wonder how I can correct this?

ANSWER

Coming above the bit is an effort to evade the correct pressure of the bit. It may happen for a variety of reasons.

The rider may be failing to use the legs sufficiently to push the horse forwards into a contact.

The contact may be too hard or too loose for the horse to be able to accept.

The horse may be unhappy about the type of bit used or it may be badly fitted.

Insufficient preparation for a movement or sudden aids can cause the horse to fling his head up. Nervous or excitable horses are rather prone to coming above the bit unless ridden carefully.

Horses will sometimes come above the bit if their balance is such that they feel the necessity to move the head and neck to save themselves. They may actually be pulled above the bit, by poor riding, resulting from insecurity of the seat of the rider, who uses the reins for his own balance.

Good co-ordination of hands and legs will be important to the correction of coming above the bit.

Question
I am told that my horse has a one-sided mouth. What does this mean?

ANSWER
It means that he responds to the rein aid on one side better than the other.

When the rein is applied, the horse's mouth is softer to the hand on the side to which he will bend. It has probably come about by the rider being unaware of the importance of making the horse equally supple on both reins.

We often make our horses one-sided by being one-sided ourselves, using a) inconsistent pressure to one side, or b) constantly using a restricting pressure on one side. Consider whether you come into either of these categories.

To correct the one-sidedness, work should be done on the harder side of the mouth to soften it, using flexions and correct bend.

In future a more equal use of the aids will prevent the mouth becoming hard on one side again.

Question
I have quite a lot of trouble with my horse crossing his jaw especially in downward transitions. Why does he do it and how can I stop him?

ANSWER
Your horse is crossing his jaw in order to evade the correct acceptance of the bit.

It will happen more in the downward transitions if he is asked with more rein than leg. He will need to learn to accept the aids more evenly.

One exercise that will help to improve matters will be flexions to each side to loosen the jaw and poll which the horse may be using to aid his resistance. The flexion should occur where the head joins the neck not further back. The horse should soften in his mouth to each hand before the other flexion is taken, the whole operation being done slowly and gently.

Force should not be used because it will result in more resistance.

Question
My horse seems to hold his head nicely and is very light, but I have been told he is 'behind the bit'. What does this mean?

ANSWER
If your horse is indeed behind the bit, then he is not truly accepting it.

This way of cheating the correct acceptance can be quite a big problem to correct if the horse has done it for some time. It sometimes leads to overbending when the horse evades the bit even more by bringing his nose into his chest.

It can be quite a clever evasion and can fool the rider because he feels light in the mouth. It is not until the horse is asked to do something more difficult, or to accept more impulsion, that the problem becomes apparent.

I think that the first thing to do is to make sure that your horse is going well forward from the leg. This energy should travel through the horse and arrive at the front, then it will have to be controlled.

If the acceptance is correct the horse will take the bit and ask to go forward, with his head and neck stretching towards it, not pulling or grabbing but allowing himself to be connected elastically. Any drawing backwards of the neck or nose will indicate that it is necessary to ride more firmly from the leg to create more impulsion.

Transitions will also be a help to improving this problem

but it will not be solved unless the rider maintains a firm contact, so that the horse learns not to avoid it.

Question
I am very worried because my horse has started grinding his teeth. Is there anything I should do?

ANSWER
If your horse has been working satisfactorily and has just begun to grind his teeth, it may be because he is worried about some new exercise you are attempting.

If this is the case, try to assess whether the work is too difficult at the moment, or whether you could make it easier by asking less for a few days. If you feel that you must pursue the exercise try to keep him as calm as you can because grinding is usually caused by anxiety. Also, check that your aids are correct and clear. Once an exercise is fully understood, grinding will usually stop and, similarly, once the aids are fully accepted, the horse will relax and cease grinding.

Sometimes, unfortunately, the problem continues, or repeats itself with every new piece of work. This can be very difficult or almost impossible to correct, the horse having developed a habit.

Question
I was schooling my horse one day and he suddenly twitched his ears quite violently and then did not seem to want to go forwards. Can you tell me why this might be?

ANSWER
There are times during training when this can happen. It could be to do with flies, which some horses hate more than others, but may be due to the difficulty of the exercise.

I think there are two main causes.

1. Any exercise requiring more bend, more impulsion or

collection could cause some strain of the poll area. This could panic the horse or even cause him some pain. He reacts by ear twitching or even appearing to drop one ear lower than the other. It may last a moment or two, or even longer. The rider should immediately ease the pressure and ride more freely forward. After a few minutes the horse will relax and all will be well. The exercise may be repeated that day but to a lesser degree.

2. The second cause is over-restriction by the hands of the rider, in which case it will be necessary to learn to be more sympathetic. Contact with the mouth should always be a feel and ease process, not a continuous grip.

One other word of warning regarding ears. It is very unwise to try to investigate a problem inside the ear because much damage could be done. If you are worried, call in your veterinary surgeon.

Question
My horse never seems to have his ears forward when I am schooling. Is he bored?

ANSWER
Well of course he certainly could be! It depends on what you are doing.

Schooling should not be boring to the horse if his mind is kept interested, and he is actually working. Riders should use school exercises intelligently, choosing some which are suitable to the horse's standard.

Work on an exercise until some improvement is made and then reward the horse by giving a brief rest on a long rein. Then work on the next exercise and so on.

Keep his mind alive by making him go forwards and by using the fingers to make conversation with the mouth. Try to avoid kicking him along which must be very boring for him. Also 'dead' hands are likely to kill interest in school work.

If the horse is learning and being rewarded for doing so, he will be more cheerful.

There are, I admit, a few horses that simply do not prick their ears however good their riders are, or however interesting the work may be. Fortunately they are in the minority because I have found no real answer to this. They usually seem quite happy, and work well, but simply do not put their ears forward. If your horse is like this, he may not actually be bored, but just likes to carry them like that?

Question
My horse keeps tilting his head to the right. What can I do?

ANSWER
There can be several reasons for a horse tilting his head.

The rider's hands may be the cause. Uneven contact, restricting hands, or hands too 'set' may make the horse unhappy enough to look for an evasion to the pressure of the bit.

Incorrect training may cause tilting. All through training the rider must be very aware of keeping his horse straight through the reins. If he allows stiffness to develop from poor use of the school exercises the horse will be less comfortable on one particular rein and tilting may result. Insufficient use of the legs to create energy into the bridle may cause the problem.

Sometimes there can be something wrong in the horse's mouth such as a sharp tooth or, in the case of a young horse, changing teeth.

Whatever the cause, if the head continually, or occasionally, tilts, the following would be the normal procedure.

Keep the contact on the side to which the nose tilts and use a feel and ease process with the fingers on the other hand. After a while this should draw the head to an even position. If the mouth remains hard on the side to which the head is tilting, an alternate pressure on each side of the mouth may help to achieve softening.

Firm use of the rider's legs is essential to any correction.

Question

I have a lot of trouble with my horse shaking his head. What can I do to keep it still?

ANSWER

The first thing to discover is whether your horse is simply being resistant to the aids, which on the whole is usually the case. It may take some time to find this out because teaching horses submission to leg and hand can be a lengthy process, particularly if the rider is a novice. Less knowledgeable riders take time to learn to co-ordinate their legs and hands, and unless their aids are correct and consistent, the horse may be slightly, or even very, unsteady.

However, there are a few horses who suffer from head shaking due to a physiological problem. I know that there has been a good deal of research into this problem but, to date, the solution has not been conclusive. I have known some head shakers to have been relieved or cured by treatment.

The very bad cases are a different matter and the best thing to do is to have veterinary advice. Such horses may be better employed in a sphere other than dressage where, although irritating, their behaviour cannot lose marks.

Question

I can't seem to stop my horse pulling. What do you suggest I do?

ANSWER

The first thing to do is to try to assess the reason for him pulling. There may be several, but the prime one could be lack of balance (on the forehand); he may be using your hands to support himself.

Lack of correct training will also cause pulling. During

training one of the first things to achieve is the establishing of a speed for each gait. Once the horse knows what is expected he will give up trying to go faster; pullers often have an impatient temperament and try to snatch the reins from the rider.

If taught to accept the aids, i.e. legs and hands for control, he will not be able to pull. Riders often make the mistake of pulling back. This really can only aggravate the problem and, since the horse's strength is so much greater, is futile in any case.

Riders must achieve better control by learning the correct use of the aids, and how to put the horse on the bit.

In the case of the horse pulling because he is on the fore-hand, the rider would need to know how and when to use a half halt to correct the balance.

Some work done on the lunge with side reins can be a big help in teaching the horse to carry himself at a slower speed.

Question

In trot my horse keeps putting me on the same diagonal. What should I do?

ANSWER

I believe that this problem occurs owing to the one-sided-ness, or stiffness, of the horse.

A stiff horse normally has one side to which he curves willingly, and one to which he does not. The stride in the curved side will often be shorter, which will be less comfortable for both horse and rider, therefore the rider will probably automatically ride on the diagonal of the longer stride and often the horse will bump a novice rider onto the diagonal which is best for him.

Try to improve the problem by disciplining yourself to change diagonals every ten strides or so, both to accustom yourself to the feel of each diagonal and to gradually even up the horse's muscles.

School exercises will, in time, make the horse more

supple which will improve matters.

Question
At home my horse is really nice to ride, but when I take him to a show he behaves like a lunatic. Is he unsuitable for competition?

ANSWER
I would think that probably you need to take your horse on many more outings in company until the show scene excites him less. Alternatively, it may be that his training is not yet sufficient to give the necessary control at a show, in which case time to gain more obedience is required. Just because he is good at home does not mean that he is sufficiently trained. Perhaps he needs to get to a higher stage before you try again.

Question
Several times my horse has bolted with me. Can you tell me what to do?

ANSWER
Before I answer this question I think we should be clear as to exactly what bolting is.

It means to me that the horse is totally out of control, either from fright or because he is incorrectly trained. He runs 'blind', not really knowing what he is doing, and may take the rider over or through any obstacle in his way, which is extremely dangerous.

If a horse escapes the aids for a short time, I would not class this as bolting. The best remedy of course would be never to allow it to happen! This may be easier said than done, but if you know what might set off the problem, it should, with care, be possible to avoid it.

The more obedient a horse is, the easier it is to solve difficulties. This means patient training to teach them to respect and answer the aids, preferably in an enclosed area, until they know that they must obey the rider. Then, even in a tricky situation out in the open, you will have a better chance of maintaining control.

Question
My horse has developed a nasty habit of rearing when he does not want to do something. What can I do?

ANSWER
Rearing is probably the nastiest evasion of all. The horse has unfortunately discovered that by doing this he can get away from your aids and he has you at his mercy. There are ways of correcting a rearer which I really cannot go into in this book because they are best dealt with by very experienced riders. You may be forced to take him to someone who can sort him out if you cannot overcome the problem yourself.

In the meantime, perhaps you should try going back to the beginning in order to teach the horse the aids all over again. He must go forwards when told and this is the main thing to concentrate on. He will not be able to come on the bit until he does, so get him to go forward at all costs and worry about the front end later.

Question
In a competition recently I was marked down because my horse was unlevel. When I enquired what this meant I was told he might have some trouble 'high up'. What did this mean and what can I do about it?

ANSWER
The term 'unlevel' is used when the stride is not quite even, either in front or behind. The horse can appear to be lame at times, or possibly all the time.

'High up' is an expression used when the horse is unlevel behind and will refer to the possibility of there being something wrong in the back. This could be a fusion of two or more vertebrae due to arthritis or injury, or it could be a muscular problem. If it is the latter, it may be due to uneven development or a strain.

In the case of uneven development, better use of the training exercises correctly executed, can improve or cure the problem, but it may take considerable time.

A strain is obviously a veterinary problem and should be dealt with accordingly.

In the case of fusion, which can be discovered by the use of X-ray, advice will again be given by the veterinary surgeon as to the horse's future use.

Question

How do I know when I have enough impulsion?

ANSWER

This is difficult to answer specifically because the required impulsion varies from novice to advanced work and may do so from one movement to another.

In general, therefore, you may assess this from the ease with which the horse performs. If he labours through his work he probably does not have enough. If he appears to be constantly fighting to go faster he has too much or at any rate it is misplaced. Impulsion is the result of being balanced and active with the hindquarters well engaged. It then has to be contained through suppleness and acceptance of the aids. If this is taking place the horse will be able to operate easily through any movement you wish to perform.

Question

Can you tell me which way my horse should be bent during a 5 m loop up the side of the arena in trot or in canter, do I change the bend or not?

ANSWER

In trot, the bend should be changed through the loop according to the direction. In canter, the bend remains towards the leading leg throughout.

Question

What exactly does covering ground mean?

ANSWER

A ground-covering stride is one which makes ground in the moments of suspension. If a horse does not have naturally good suspension in trot and canter he will have far more difficulty than one who does. Increasing the engagement of the hindquarters and impulsion should help to prolong the moment of suspension.

Question

On my dressage sheets I am being constantly told that my horse is 'short in the neck'. Is this a conformation fault or a training one?

ANSWER

Some horses are of course built short in the neck but this comment will have been used to mean that either you are restricting freedom by incorrect use of the hands or you are tying to collect the horse by drawing him together with your hands instead of engaging his hindquarters with your seat and legs to bring him to the correct outline.

Question

What does a judge mean when he says my horse is not 'between hand and leg'?

ANSWER

The aids that you give your horse to ask him to respond to

your requests are a combined operation, i.e. your leg aids ask the horse to go forward and your hands control the result. If there is a break in that co-ordination by an inconsistant pressure of the leg or a drop in the rein contact there will be a loophole through which the horse can escape the aids. He may use it to take control, enabling him to do what he wants which can cause all manner of problems.

Question

Judges seem to vary as to how they want to see the horse go. If I find that a judge has a particular 'hate' should I adjust my test to please him or her?

ANSWER

If you find a judge who does not seem to like the way your horse goes you should find out whether he has a valid point or not! This may be done with the help of a trainer or some established expert who has proved themself in the arena. If you are satisfied that your training is taking you in the direction you want to go, even if it does not please the judge, do not on any account make any alterations. This will only cause confusion between you and your horse and could set your training back. The best advice I can give is to avoid that judge in future!

Question

When executing a flying change I have trouble keeping my horse straight. He always tries to throw himself to the left. What do you advise?

ANSWER

It is always difficult to give answers without seeing the problem, but I think you have to work through a checklist. Are you sitting correctly in the change, or are you twisting your body or coming out of the saddle? Do you have adequate control of the horse between the inside leg and the outside hand? Are you riding a line looking ahead to the marker at which you want to arrive?

So often the control of a basic straightness is faulty which can allow stiffness to develop. Any one-sidedness may cause problems. A shoulder-in position is very helpful in controlling the straightness but sometimes an outward flexion taken for a a few strides will ensure that the horse cannot bring his weight onto his shoulders to evade the normal aids.

Question
My pony always stops to dung and I cannot prevent it, I am not sure what to do.

ANSWER
I am afraid that the answer may seem very callous but I have to advise you to give him a sharp aid, or several if necessary, with a schooling whip at the same time as your legs. He may resent this but must learn not to do it because it will be a nuisance in competition and can actually be quite dangerous if he happens to want to perform when there are horses behind you or when you are in traffic.